CH00905015

Situational and Professional Responsibility Q&A

A pocket guide of questions and answers about the more difficult topics on the PMP® exam

Rita Mulcahy, PMP

RMC Publications, Inc.

ISBN: 0-9711647-4-6

Printed in the USA

First printing, January 2002

Published by:
RMC Publications, Inc.

Phone: 952-846-4484
Email: info@rmcproject.com
Web: www.rmcproject.com

TABLE OF CONTENTS

Introduction	4
How to Study Using This Book	5
What Materials to Use to Study	6
Framework Questions	11
Integration Questions	50
Scope Questions	66
Time Questions	77
Cost Questions	94
Quality Questions	106
Human Resource Questions	118
Communications Questions	129
Risk Questions	141
Procurement Questions	152

INTRODUCTION

The more than 75 situational questions on the PMP® exam have troubled thousands of the project managers I have helped obtain PMP® certification. These questions are among the most difficult because they require the test taker to ANALYZE a situation and APPLY project management knowledge.

Now, to add to this anxiety, professional responsibility has become more emphasized on the exam. It is not in the 2000 Edition of the PMBOK® Guide nor is it mentioned in many other sources. (It is covered here and in the PMP® simulation software, *PM FASTrack™.*)

I created this supplement to the book PMP® Exam Prep to provide practice with situational and professional responsibility questions.

PLEASE NOTE: The questions contained in this book are a small subset of the 1,300 questions on the PMP® Simulation CD-ROM called *PM FASTrack™.*

HOW TO STUDY USING THIS BOOK

I suggest that you use this book AFTER you have studied the book *PMP® Exam Prep* and are ready for more difficult questions.

To be successful at answering the wordier questions on the exam, you must first interpret what topic the question is asking about, then determine what knowledge to apply.

Here is one of the tricks from the book *PMP® Exam Prep* for answering long, wordy questions:
1. Find the actual question in the data or situation.
2. Identify the topic being asked about (schedule development, time, cost, conflict resolution, changes) and any descriptors (first, last, best, not, except).
3. Read the entire question, ignoring any information not relevant to the question.
4. Come up with an answer.
5. Compare your answer to choice D, then C, B and A until you discover the correct or "best" answer.

WHAT MATERIALS TO USE TO STUDY

You will need other materials to get ready for the exam in addition to this book! The following have been used successfully by thousands of people.

PMP® EXAM PREP, THIRD EDITION
(2001) ISBN: 0-9711647-0-3

 Used by thousands as the primary study tool for passing the exam, this book contains 224 pages of explanations of core concepts (including topics that have been driving you crazy—like network diagrams, slack, and earned value), exercises and games. Also included are insider tips on how to study, what to study, and how to take the exam. This book has been called a "must read!"

PM FASTRACK™ - PMP® SIMULATION SOFTWARE

(CD-ROM, 2001)
ISBN: 0-9711647-1-1

 One of the three key products for passing the exam, use this program to practice computerized testing and work through 1,300 questions in four testing modes. Not only does this PMP® simulation software program have more questions in more modes than any other CD available, but it was also created based on a psychometric review and sorts questions **LIKE THE ACTUAL EXAM!**

HOT TOPICS FLASHCARDS
Book **or** Audio CD Version
ISBN: 0-9711647-2-X

This "must have" item is a portable tool for improving the recall and understanding you will need to answer even situational questions on the PMP® and CAPM® exams. Simply read (or hear) the Hot Topic on the front of each of the 650 pages and see if you can recall all the items on the back of the page (or as read back to you), as well as know what they mean.

PMP EXAM PREP CLASSES

"This is the best course I have ever taken on ANY subject!"

"I loved the book but this class provided so much more!"

"Your expertise shows!"

"I feel ready to take the exam TODAY!"

- 2 days long with a 99% success rate

- Decrease study time to 40 hours or less

- Receive insider tips

- Understand the vital material on the exam that is not in the 2000 Edition of the PMBOK® Guide

PMI approved! Many PMI chapters who want expert instruction and the best material have selected this course.

OTHER TRAINING: See our other project management classes to meet the 35-hour training requirement to take the PMP® and CAPM® exams or advanced classes to gain PDU's for maintaining your certification.

www.rmcproject.com

SITUATIONAL AND PROFESSIONAL RESPONSIBILITY

QUESTIONS

FRAMEWORK QUESTIONS

1. Near the end of your last project, additional requirements were demanded by a group of stakeholders when they learned they would be affected by your project. This became a problem because you had not included the time or cost in the project plan to perform these requirements. What is the BEST thing you can do to prevent such a problem on future projects?

    A. Review the WBS dictionary more thoroughly, looking for incomplete descriptions

    B. Review the charter more thoroughly, examining the business case for "holes"

    C. Pay more attention to stakeholder management

    D. Do a more thorough job of solicitation planning

2. The software development project is not going well. There are over 30 stakeholders, and no one can agree on the project objectives. One stakeholder believes the project can achieve a 30% improvement while another believes a 50% improvement is possible. The project manager thinks a 10% improvement is more realistic. What is the BEST course of action?

A. Move forward with the project and hope more information comes to light later to settle the issue

B. Average the numbers and use that as the goal

C. Perform a feasibility analysis

D. Ask the sponsor to make the final decision

3. **Your management has decided that all orders will be treated as "projects" and that project managers will be used to update orders daily, resolving issues and ensuring that the customer formally accepts the product within 30 days of completion. The revenue from the individual orders can vary from US $100 to US $150,000. The project manager will not be required to perform planning or provide documentation other than daily status. How would you define this situation?**

A. Because each individual order is a "temporary endeavor," each order is a project. This is truly project management.

B. This is program management since there are multiple projects involved.

C. This is a recurring process.

D. Orders incurring revenue over US $100,000 would be considered projects and would involve project management.

4. **A project manager's boss and the head of engineering discuss a change to a major task. After the meeting, the boss contacts the project manager and tells him to make the change. This is an example of:**

A. management attention to scope management.

B. management planning.

C. a project coordinator position.

D. a change control system.

5. **A project team has completed all the technical project deliverables, and the customer has accepted the deliverables. However, the lessons learned required by the project office have not been completed. What is the status of the project?**

A. The project is incomplete because the project needs to be re-planned.

B. The project is incomplete until all deliverables are complete and accepted.

C The project is complete because the customer has accepted the deliverables.

D. The project is complete because the project has reached the due date.

6. **You are in the middle of a new product development project for your publicly traded company when you discover that the previous project manager made a US $3,000,000 payment that was not approved in accordance with your company policies. Luckily, the project CPI is 1.2. What should you do?**

A. Bury the cost in the largest cost center available

B. Put the payment in an escrow account

C. Contact your manager

D. Ignore the payment

7. **While preparing your risk responses, you realize that you have not planned for unknown risk events. You need to make adjustments to the project to compensate for unknown risk events. These adjustments are based on your past project experience when unknown risk events occurred and knocked the project off track. What should you do?**

   A. Apply a general contingency to try to compensate

   B. Document the unknown risk items and calculate the expected monetary value based on probability and impact that result from the occurrence

   C. Determine the unknown risk events and the associated cost, then add the cost to the project budget as reserves

   D. Add a 10% contingency

8. **During a meeting with some of the project stakeholders, the project manager is asked to add work to the project scope of work. The project manager had access to correspondence about the project before the charter was signed and remembers that the project sponsors specifically denied the scope of work mentioned by these stakeholders. The BEST thing for the project manager to do would be to:**

A. let the sponsors know of the stakeholders' request.

B. evaluate the impact of adding the scope of work.

C. tell the stakeholders the scope cannot be added.

D. add the work if there is time available in the project schedule.

9. **When checking a calendar of a team member to schedule a meeting, you see she has scheduled a meeting with a key stakeholder that you were not informed of. The BEST approach would be to:**

A. avoid mentioning it to the team member but continue to watch their activities.

B. notify your boss about the problem.

C. address the concern with the team member.

D. address the concern with the team member's boss.

10. The project manager is having a very difficult time keeping a project schedule on track. The project is 13 months long and requires 220 people to complete. All of the project problems have been fixed to the project manager's satisfaction, the SPI is currently .67, the CPI is 1.26, there are 23 tasks on the critical path, and the project PERT duration is 26. Under these circumstances, the monthly status report should say that the project:

A. has too many people assigned to it.

B. is behind schedule.

C. cost is behind budget.

D. is too risky.

11. **Your employee is three days late with a report. Five minutes before the meeting where the topic of the report is to be discussed, she hands you the report. You notice some serious errors in it. What should you do?**

A. Cancel the meeting and reschedule when the report is fixed

B. Go to the meeting and tell the other attendees there are errors in the report

C. Force the employee to do the presentation and remain silent as the other attendees find the errors

D. Cancel the meeting and rewrite the report yourself

12. **While completing a project, a project manager realizes he needs to decrease project costs. After researching his options, he comes up with the following choices. Which choice would DECREASE project costs?**

A. Change to component A from component B. Component A costs more to purchase but has a lower life-cycle cost than B.

B. Change task A to be completed by resource B instead of resource C. Resource B is a more experienced worker.

C. Move tasks B and H to occur concurrently, and take the risk of a 30% increase in the need for five more resources later.

D. Delete an acceptance test from the project plan.

13. A manager has been given responsibility for a project that has the support of senior management. From the beginning, you have disagreed with the manager as to how the project should proceed and what the deliverables should be. You and she have disagreed over many issues in the past. Your department has been tasked with providing some key tasks for the project. What should you do?

A. Provide the manager with what she needs

B. Inform your manager of your concerns to get their support

C. Sit down with the manager at the beginning of the project and attempt to describe why you object to the project and discover a way to solve the problem

D. Ask to be removed from the project

14. **A large, complex construction project in a foreign country requires coordination to move the required equipment through crowded city streets. To ensure the equipment is transported successfully, your contact in that country informs you that you will have to pay the local police a fee for coordinating traffic. What should you do?**

A. Do not pay the fee because it is a bribe

B. Eliminate the task

C. Pay the fee

D. Do not pay the fee if it is not part of the project estimate

15. **A major negotiation with a potential subcontractor is scheduled for tomorrow when you discover there is a good chance the project will be canceled. What should you do?**

A. Do not spend too much time preparing for the negotiations

B. Cut the negotiations short

C. Only negotiate major items

D. Postpone the negotiations

16. **You've been assigned to take over managing a project that should be half-complete according to the schedule. You discover that the project is running far behind schedule, and that the project will probably take double the time originally estimated by the previous project manager. However, upper management has been told that the project is on schedule. What is the BEST course of action?**

A. Try to restructure the schedule to meet the project deadline

B. Report your assessment to upper management

C. Turn the project back to the previous project manager

D. Move forward with the schedule as planned by the previous project manager and report at the first missed milestone

17. You are halfway through a major network rollout. There are 300 locations in the U.S. with another 20 in England. A software seller has just released a major software upgrade for some of the equipment being installed. The upgrade would provide the customer with functionality they requested that was not available at the time the project began. What is the BEST course of action under these circumstances?

A. Continue as planned, your customer has not requested a change

B. Inform the customer of the upgrade and the impacts to the project's timeline and functionality

C. Implement the change and adjust the schedule as necessary because this supports the customer's original request

D. Implement the change to the remaining sites and continue with the schedule

18. You are working on your research and development project when your customer asks you to include a particular component in the project. You know this represents new work, and you do not have excess funds available. What should you do?

A. Delete another lower priority task to make more time and funds available

B. Use funds from the management reserve to cover the cost

C. Follow the contract change control process

D. Ask for more funds from the project sponsor

19. You are a project manager for one of many projects in a large and important program. At a high-level status meeting, you note that another project manager has reported her project on schedule. Looking back on your project over the last few weeks, you remember many deliverables from the other project that arrived late. What should you do?

A. Meet with the program manager

B. Develop a risk control plan

C. Discuss the issues with your boss

D. Meet with the other project manager

20. You have always been asked by your management to cut your project estimate by 10% after you have given it to them. The scope of your new project is unclear and there are over 30 stakeholders. Management expects a 25% reduction in downtime as a result of the project. Which of the following is the BEST course of action in this situation?

A. Re-plan to achieve a 35% improvement

B. Reduce the estimates and note the changes in the risk management plan

C. Provide an accurate estimate of the actual costs and be able to support it

D. Meet with the team to identify where you can find 10% savings

21. Your employee is three days late with a report. She walks into a meeting where the report is to be discussed and hands you a copy five minutes before the topic is to be discussed. You notice some serious errors in the report. How could this have been prevented?

A. Require periodic updates from the employee

B. Coach and mentor the employee

C. Make sure the employee was competent to do the work

D. Cancel the meeting earlier because you have not had a chance to review the report

22. You are in the middle of a project when you discover that a software seller for your project is having major difficulty keeping employees due to a labor dispute. Many other projects in your company are using the company's services. What should you do?

A. Attempt to keep the required people on your project

B. Tell the other project managers in your company about the labor problem

C. Contact the company and advise it that you will cancel its work on the project unless it settles its labor dispute

D. Cease doing business with the company

23. **All of the following are the responsibility of a project manager EXCEPT?**

A. Maintain the confidentiality of customer confidential information

B. Determine the legality of company procedures

C. Ensure that a legal conflict of interest does not compromise the legitimate interest of the customer

D. Provide accurate and truthful representations in cost estimates

24. In order to complete work on your projects, you have been provided confidential information from all of your clients. A university contacts you to help it in its research. Such assistance would require you to provide it with some of the client data from your files. What should you do?

A. Release the information, but remove all references to the client's name

B. Provide high level information only

C. Contact your clients and seek permission to disclose the information

D. Disclose the information

25. You just found out that a major subcontractor for your project consistently provides deliverables late. The subcontractor approaches you and asks you to continue accepting late deliverables in exchange for a decrease in project costs. This offer is an example of:

A. confrontation.

B. compromise.

C. smoothing.

D. forcing.

26. Management has promised you part of the incentive fee from the customer if you complete the project early. Later, while finalizing a major deliverable, your team informs you that the deliverable meets the requirements in the contract but will not provide the functionality the customer needs. If the deliverable is late, the project will not be completed early. What action should you take?

A. Provide the deliverable as it is

B. Inform the customer of the situation and work out a mutually agreeable solution

C. Start to compile a list of delays caused by the buyer to prepare for negotiations

D. Cut other tasks in a way that will be unnoticed to provide more time to fix the deliverable

27. **You have just discovered an error in the implementation plan that will prevent you from meeting a milestone date. The BEST thing you can do is:**

A. develop alternative solutions to meet the milestone date.

B. change the milestone date.

C. remove any discussion about due dates in the project status report.

D. educate the team about the need to meet milestone dates.

28. While testing the strength of concrete poured on your project, you discover that over 35% of the concrete does not meet your company's quality standards. You feel certain the concrete will function as it is, and you don't think the concrete needs to meet the quality level specified. What should you do?

A. Change the quality standards to meet the level achieved

B. List in your reports that the concrete simply "meets our quality needs"

C. Ensure the remaining concrete meets the standard

D. Report the lesser quality level and try to find a solution

29. You are the project manager for a new international project, and your project team includes people from four countries. Most of the team members have not worked on similar projects before, but the project has strong support from senior management. What is the BEST thing to do to ensure that cultural differences do not interfere with the project?

A. Spend a little more time creating the work breakdown structure and making sure it is complete

B. As the project manager, make sure you choose your words carefully whenever you communicate

C. Ask one person at each team meeting to describe something unique about their culture

D. Carefully encode all the project manager's communications

30. **A project has a tight budget when you begin negotiating with a seller for a piece of equipment. The seller has told you that the equipment price is fixed. Your manager has told you to negotiate the cost with the seller. What is your BEST course of action?**

A. Make a good faith effort to find a way to decrease the cost

B. Postpone negotiations until you can convince your manager to change their mind

C. Hold the negotiations but only negotiate other aspects of the project

D. Cancel the negotiations

31. You are working on a large construction project that is progressing within the baseline. Resource usage has remained steady, and your boss has just awarded you a prize for your performance. One of your team members returns from a meeting with the customer and tells you the customer said they are not happy with the project progress. What is the FIRST thing you should do?

A. Tell your manager

B. Complete a team building exercise and invite the customer's representatives

C. Change the schedule baseline

D. Meet with the customer to uncover details

32. **A project manager discovers a defect in a deliverable due to the customer under contract today. The project manager knows the customer does not have the technical understanding to notice the defect. The deliverable technically meets the contract requirements, but it does not meet the project manager's fitness of use standard. What should the project manager do in this situation?**

A. Issue the deliverable and get formal acceptance from the customer

B. Note the problem in the lessons learned so future projects do not encounter the same problem

C. Discuss the issue with the customer

D. Inform the customer that the deliverable will be late

33. You have just been assigned as project manager for a new telecommunications project. There appear to be many risks on this project, but no one has evaluated them to assess the range of possible project outcomes. What needs to be done?

A. Risk identification

B. Risk quantification

C. Risk response planning

D. Risk monitoring and control

34. **Management tells a project manager to subcontract part of the project to a company that management has worked with many times. Under these circumstances, the project manager should be MOST concerned about:**

A. making sure the company has the qualifications to complete the project.

B. meeting management expectations of time.

C. the cost of the subcontracted work.

D. the contract terms and conditions.

35. The customer on a project tells the project manager he has run out of money to pay for the project. What should the project manager do FIRST?

A. Shift more of the work to later in the schedule to allow time for the customer to get the funds

B. Reduce the scope of work and enter closure

C. Stop work

D. Release part of the project team

36. You are the project manager for a large project under contract with the government. The contract for this two year, multi-million dollar project was signed six months ago. You were not involved in contract negotiations or setting up procedures for managing changes, but now you are swamped with changes from the sponsor and from people inside your organization. Who is normally responsible for formally reviewing major changes to the project/contract?

A. The change control board

B. The contracting/legal department

C. The project manager

D. Senior management

37. **During execution, a major problem occurred that was not included in the risk response plan. What should you do FIRST?**

A. Create a workaround

B. Reevaluate the risk identification process

C. Look for any unexpected effects of the problem

D. Tell management

38. **During planning, a project manager discovers that part of the scope of work is undefined. What should the project manager do?**

A. Continue to plan for the project until the scope of work is defined

B. Remove the scope of work from the project and include it in the upgrade to the project

C. Issue a change to the project when the scope is defined

D. Ask management to help get the work defined

39. The engineering department wants the project objective to be a 10% improvement in throughput. The information technology department wants no more than 5% of its resources to be used on the project. The sponsor, who is also your boss, wants the project team to decrease tax liability. The BEST thing you can do is:

A. put a plan together that meets all the objectives.

B. have these people get together and agree on one objective.

C. include the engineering and information technology objectives but hold further meetings regarding the sponsor's objectives.

D. include only the sponsor's requirements.

INTEGRATION QUESTIONS

40. **The previous project manager for your project managed it without much project organization. There is a lack of management control and no clearly defined project deliverables. Which of the following would be the BEST choice for getting your project better organized?**

A. Adopt a life-cycle approach to the project

B. Develop lessons learned for each phase

C. Develop specific work plans for each phase of the project

D. Develop a description of the product of the project

41. You are taking over a project during the planning phase and discover that six individuals have signed the project charter. Which of the following should MOST concern you?

A. The charter was created during planning

B. Spending more time on configuration management

C. Getting a single project sponsor

D. Determining the reporting structure

42. **The project charter for a project was approved for planning, and you have just been assigned as project manager. Realizing that planning is an ongoing effort throughout the project life-cycle, which core processes are you MOST likely to combine?**

A. Scope definition and activity definition

B. Activity duration estimating and schedule development

C. Resource planning and cost estimating

D. Cost estimating and cost budgeting

43. You have never managed a project before and are asked to plan a new project. It would be BEST in this situation to rely on _____ during planning to improve your chance of success.

A. your management skills

B. your previous training

C. historical records

D. responsibility charts

44. A project manager is appointed to head a highly technical project in an area with which this person has limited familiarity. The project manager delegates schedule development, cost estimating, selection of tasks, and assignments to work activities to various project team members, and basically serves as an occasional referee and coordinator of activities. The results of this approach are likely to be:

A. a team functioning throughout the project at a very high level and demonstrating creativity and commitment.

B. a team that initially experiences some amounts of confusion, but that after a period of time becomes a cohesive and effective unit.

C. a team that is not highly productive, but that stays together because of the work environment created by the project manager.

D. a team that is characterized by poor performance, low morale, high levels of conflict, and high turnover.

45. You are in the middle of executing a major modification to an existing product when you learn that the resources promised at the beginning of the project are not available. The BEST thing to do is to:

A. show how the resources were originally promised to your project and request that they be moved back to your project.

B. re-plan the project without the resources.

C. explain what will happen if the resources are not made available.

D. crash the project.

46. You have been assigned to manage the development of an organization's first website. The site will be highly complex and interactive, and neither your project team nor the client has much experience with website development. The timeline is extremely aggressive. Any delay will be costly for both your firm and the client. You have an executive sponsor and have achieved agreement and sign-off on both the project charter and the project plan. Client personnel have been kept fully informed of the project's progress through status reports and regular meetings. The project is on schedule, within the budget, and a final perfunctory review has been scheduled. Suddenly, you hear that the entire effort may be cancelled, because the product developed is totally unacceptable. What is the MOST likely cause of this situation?

A. A key stakeholder was not adequately involved in the project.

B. The project charter and project plan were not thoroughly explained or adequately reviewed by the client.

C. Communication arrangements were inadequate and did not provide the required information to interested parties.

D. The executive sponsor failed to provide adequate support for the project.

47. **The project manager has just received a change from the customer that does not affect project time and is easy to complete. What should the project manager do FIRST?**

A. Make the change happen as soon as possible

B. Contact the project sponsor for permission

C. Go to the change control board

D. Evaluate the other components of the triple constraint

48. Your company just won a major new project. It will begin in three months and is valued at US $2,000,000. You are the project manager for an existing project. What is the FIRST thing you should do once you hear of the new project?

A. Ask management how the new project will use resources

B. Resource level your project

C. Crash your project

D. Ask management how the new project will affect your project

49. You are a project manager who was just assigned to take over a project from another project manager who is leaving the company. The old project manager tells you that the project is on schedule only because he has had to constantly push the team to perform. What is the FIRST thing you should do as the new project manager?

A. Check risk status

B. Check cost performance

C. Determine a management strategy

D. Tell the team your objectives

50. You are assigned to be the project manager in the middle of the project. The project is within tolerances for the baseline, but the customer is not happy with the performance of the project. What is the FIRST thing you should do?

A. Discuss it with the project team

B. Recalculate baselines

C. Renegotiate the contract

D. Meet with the customer

51. **A project manager learns that corrective action was taken by a team member and was not documented. What should the project manager do NEXT?**

A. Report the violation to the functional manager

B. Clarify the reasoning behind the team member's action

C. Ask if the action should be documented

D. Find out who caused the problem

52. The client demands changes to the product specification that will add two weeks to the critical path. The project manager should:

A. crash the project to recover the two weeks.

B. fast track the project to recover the two weeks.

C. consult management before proceeding.

D. advise the client of the impact of the change.

53. During the execution of a project, the project manager determines that a change is needed to material purchased for the project. The project manager calls a team meeting to plan how to make the change. This action is an example of:

A. management by objectives.

B. lack of a change control system.

C. good team relations.

D. lack of a clear work breakdown structure.

54. **What should a project manager do FIRST if a team member has added functionality to a product in the project without impacting time, cost, and schedule?**

A. Ask the team member how the need for the functionality was determined

B. Ask the finance department to assess the value of the improvement

C. Ask the customer to review this and to submit a change request

D. Ask the team member how they know there is no time, cost, or schedule impact

55. A team member notifies you, after the fact, that she has added extra functionality to the project. There was no impact on the cost or schedule. What should be done as a result of this change?

A. Inform the customer

B. Make sure marketing is aware of the change

C. Understand what functionality was added

D. Implement change control processes to track the change

SCOPE QUESTIONS

56. The company is taking a vote to see if the contracts department should be split up and reassigned to projects or remain intact. A contract professional might not want this to occur because they would lose _____ in a decentralized contracting environment.

    A. standardized company project management practices

    B. loyalty to the project

    C. a clearly defined career path

    D. expertise

57. You are a project manager for a large consulting firm. Your superior has just asked for your input on a decision about which project your company should pursue. Project A has an internal rate of return of 12%. Project B has a predicted Benefit Cost Ratio (BCR) of 1:3. Project C has an opportunity cost of US $75,000. Project D has a payback period of six months. Based on the following, WHICH project would you recommend?

A. Project A

B. Project B

C. Project C

D. Project D

58. **A project manager has just been assigned to a new project and has been given the completed project scope. The FIRST thing the project manager must do is:**

A. create a project plan using the WBS.

B. confirm that all the stakeholders have had input to the scope of work.

C. form a team to create the procurement plan.

D. create a network diagram.

59. You have created the project charter but could not get it approved. Your manager and his boss asked that the project begin immediately. Which of the following is the BEST thing to do?

A. Set up an integrated change control process

B. Push to get the charter signed

C. Perform an impact analysis

D. Start work on only the critical path tasks

60. **A project manager is trying to convince management to use project management and has decided to start with a charter. Why would the charter help the project?**

A. It describes the details of what needs to be done.

B. It lists the names of all team members.

C. It gives the project manager authority.

D. It describes the project's history.

61. A new project manager is about to begin creating the project's scope of work. One stakeholder wants to add many items to the scope of work. Another stakeholder only wants to describe the functional requirements. The project is important for the project manager's company but a seller will do the work. Which of the following would you advise the project manager to do?

A. The scope of work should be general to allow the seller to make its own decisions.

B. The scope of work should be general to allow clarification later.

C. The scope of work should be detailed to allow clarification later.

D. The scope of work should be as detailed as necessary for the type of project.

62. The construction phase of a new software product is near completion. The next phase is testing and implementation. The project is two weeks ahead of schedule. What should the project manager be MOST concerned with before moving onto the final phase?

A. Scope verification

B. Quality control

C. Performance reports

D. Cost control

63. A customer has given you a scope of work for a complex, eight-month project that has a few unknowns. The customer has asked you to just "get it done" and only wants to see you at the end of eight months when you deliver the finished project. Under these circumstances, which of the following is the BEST thing to do?

A. Complete the project as requested, but verify its scope with the customer occasionally throughout

B. Complete the project within eight months without contacting the customer during this time

C. Ask management to check in with the customer occasionally

D. Complete the project, but document that the customer did not want contact

64. **During project execution, a project team delivers a project deliverable to the customer. However, the customer neither acknowledges the deliverable nor says if it is acceptable, although an approval is required. What is the BEST thing to do?**

A. Continue with the project

B. Document the situation

C. Contact management for help

D. Call a meeting of the team

65. **A project manager is managing a fixed price contract. She thinks that a large customer-requested change might impact the schedule of the project. What should she do FIRST?**

A. Meet with the stakeholders

B. Meet with the team

C. Renegotiate the remainder of the contract

D. Follow the change control system

66. You are managing a six month project and have held bi-weekly meetings with your project sponsors. After five-and-a-half months of work, the project is on schedule and budget, but the sponsors are not satisfied with the deliverables. This situation will delay the project completion by one month. The MOST important process that could have prevented this situation is:

A. risk monitoring and control.

B. schedule control.

C. scope planning.

D. scope change control.

67. **During activity definition, a team member identifies an activity that needs to be accomplished. However, another team member believes that the activity is not part of the project as interpreted by the project charter. What should the project manager do?**

A. Try to build a consensus of the team

B. Make the decision about inclusion herself

C. Talk with the end-user

D. Talk with the project sponsor

68. You are a project manager on a US $5,000,000 software development project. While working with your project team to develop a network diagram, you notice a series of activities that can be worked in parallel but must finish in a specific sequence. What type of activity sequencing method is required for these activities?

A. Precedence diagramming method

B. Arrow diagramming method

C. Critical path method

D. Conditional diagramming method

69. You are a project manager on a US $5,000,000 software development project. While working with your project team to develop a network diagram, your data architects suggest that quality could be improved if the data model is approved by senior management before moving on to other design elements. They support this suggestion with an article from a leading software development journal. This type of input is called a(n):

A. mandatory dependency.

B. discretionary dependency.

C. external dependency.

D. heuristic.

70. You have a project with four tasks as follows: Task 1 can start immediately and has an estimated duration of one. Task 2 can start after Task 1 is completed and has an estimated duration of four. Task 3 can start after Task 2 is completed and has an estimated duration of five. Task 4 can start after Task 1 is completed and must be completed when Task 3 is completed. The estimate for Task 4 is ten. What is the shortest amount of time in which the project can be completed?

A. 10

B. 9

C. 18

D. 11

71. **A project manager is asking team members about the time estimates for their tasks and developing agreement on the calendar date for each task. In which of the following actions is the project manager involved?**

A. Activity sequencing

B. Schedule development

C. Scope definition

D. Initiation

72. You have a project with the following tasks: Task A takes 40 hours and can start after the project starts. Task B takes 25 hours and should happen after the project starts. Task C must happen after Task A and takes 35 hours. Task D must happen after Tasks B and C and takes 30 hours. Task E must take place after Task C and takes 10 hours. Task F takes place after Task E and takes 22 hours. Which of the following is TRUE if Task B actually takes 37 hours?

A. The critical path is 67 hours.

B. The critical path changes to tasks B, D.

C. The critical path is A, C, E, F.

D. The critical path increases by 12 hours.

73. The team has provided the project manager with activity duration estimates. If the project manager is about to start schedule development, which of the following does the project manager need to adequately develop a schedule?

A. Risk management plan

B. Corrective action

C. Schedule change control system

D. Change requests

74. A project manager is taking over a project from another project manager while the project is in planning. If the new project manager wants to see what the previous project manager's plans for managing changes to the schedule were, she would look at the:

A. communication plan.

B. project plan.

C. time management plan.

D. schedule management plan.

75. **A project manager is using weighted average duration estimates to calculate activity duration. Which type of mathematical analysis is being used?**

A. CPM

B. PERT

C. Monte Carlo

D. GERT

76. The WBS, estimates for each work package, and network diagram are completed. Which of the following would be the NEXT thing for the project manager to do?

A. Sequence the activities

B. Verify that you have the correct scope of work

C. Create a preliminary schedule and get the team's approval

D. Start risk management

77. **A new product development project has four levels in the work breakdown structure and has been sequenced using the arrow diagramming method. The activity duration estimates have been received. What should be done NEXT?**

A. Create an activity list

B. Update the work breakdown structure

C. Finalize the schedule

D. Compress the schedule

78. You are a project manager for a new product development project that has four levels in the work breakdown structure, and has been sequenced using the arrow diagramming technique. The activity duration estimates have been received. What time management activity would you do NEXT?

A. Create an activity list

B. Update the work breakdown structure

C. Collect historical records

D. Duration compression

79. A team member from research and development tells you that her work is too creative to provide you with a fixed single estimate for the task. You both decide to use the average time the task has taken for past projects to predict the future. This is an example of which of the following?

A. Parametric estimating

B. PERT

C. CPM

D. Monte Carlo

80. **A task has an early start of day three, a late start of day 13, an early finish of day nine, and a late finish of day 19. The task:**

A. is on the critical path.

B. has a lag.

C. is progressing well.

D. is not on the critical path.

81. **The project is calculated to be completed four days after the desired completion date. You do not have access to additional resources. The project is low risk, the benefit cost ratio is expected to be 1.6, and the dependencies are preferential. Under these circumstances, what would be the BEST thing to do?**

A. Cut resources from a task

B. Make more tasks concurrent

C. Move resources from the preferential dependencies to the external dependencies

D. Remove a task from the project

82. A project manager for a small construction company has a project that was budgeted for US $130,000 over a six week period. According to her schedule, the project should have cost US $60,000 to date. However, it has cost US $90,000 to date. The project is also behind schedule, because the original estimates were not accurate. Who has the primarily responsibility to solve this problem?

A. Project manager

B. Senior management

C. Project sponsor

D. Manager of the project office

83. Your organization is having a difficult time managing all of its projects. You have been asked to help senior management understand this. Which of the following types of reports would help provide summary information to senior management?

A. Detailed cost estimates

B. Project plans

C. Gantt charts

D. Milestone reports

84. You have four projects from which to choose one. Project A is being done over a six year period and has an NPV (net present value) of US $70,000. Project B is being done over a three year period and has an NPV of US $30,000. Project C is being done over a five year period and has an NPV of US $40,000. Project D is being done over a one year period and has an NPV of US $60,000. Which project would you choose?

A. Project A

B. Project B

C. Project C

D. Project D

85. Project A has an IRR (internal rate of return) of 21%. Project B has an IRR of 7%. Project C has an IRR of 31%. Project D has an IRR of 19%. Which of these would be the BEST project?

A. Project A

B. Project B

C. Project C

D. Project D

86. **As a project manager, you are presented with the following information on the NPV for several potential projects. Which project is your BEST choice?**

A. Project A with an NPV of US $95,000

B. Project B with an NPV of US $120,000

C. Project C with an NPV of US $20,000

D. Project D with an NPV of -US $30,000

87. Your company can accept three possible projects. Project A has an NPV of US $30,000 and will take six years to complete. Project B has an NPV of US $60,000 and will take three years to complete. Project C has an NPV of US $90,000 and will take two years to complete. Based on this information, which project would you pick?

A. They all have the same value.

B. Project A

C. Project B

D. Project C

88. **A new store development project requires the purchase of various equipment, machinery, and furniture. The department responsible for the development recently centralized its external purchase process and standardized its new order system. In which document can these new procedures be found?**

A. Project scope statement

B. WBS

C. Staff management plan

D. Organizational policies

89. **Early in the life of your project, you are having a discussion with the sponsor about what estimating techniques should be used. You want a form of expert judgment, but the sponsor argues for analogous estimating. It would be BEST to:**

A. agree to analogous estimating as it is a form of expert judgment.

B. suggest life-cycle costing as a compromise.

C. determine why the sponsor wants such an accurate estimate.

D. try to convince the sponsor to allow expert judgment because it is typically more accurate.

90. **You've just completed the initiation phase of a small project and are moving into the planning phase when a project stakeholder asks you for the project's budget and cost baseline. What should you tell her?**

A. The project budget can be found in the project's charter, which has just been completed.

B. The project budget and baseline will not be finalized and accepted until the planning phase is completed.

C. The project plan will not contain the project's budget and baseline; this is a small project.

D. It is impossible to complete an estimate before the project plan is created.

91. The project manager is allocating overall cost estimates to individual activities or work packages to establish a baseline for measuring project performance. What step is this?

A. Cost management

B. Cost estimating

C. Cost budgeting

D. Cost control

92. **You are asked to prepare a budget for completing a project that was started last year and then shelved for six months. All the following would be included in the budget EXCEPT?**

A. Fixed cost

B. Sunk cost

C. Direct cost

D. Variable cost

93. **To accommodate a new project in your department, you need to move resources from one project to another. Because your department is currently working at capacity, moving resources will inevitably delay the project from which you move the resources. You should move resources from which of the following projects?**

A. Project A with a benefit cost ratio of .8, no project charter, and four resources

B. Project B with a net present value of US $60,000, 12 resources, and variable costs between US $1,000 and US $2,000 per month

C. Project C with an opportunity cost of US $300,000, no project control plan, and an internal rate of return of 12%

D. Project D with indirect costs of US $20,000 and 13 resources

94. **A manufacturing project has an SPI of .89 and a CPI of .91. What is the BEST explanation for why this occurred?**

A. The equipment purchased for the project was more expensive than expected.

B. At least one task has taken more time than expected.

C. Less experienced resources were used.

D. The project baseline was changed more than once.

© 2002 Rita Mulcahy, PMP. It is illegal to copy this book.

95. Although the stakeholders thought there was enough budget, halfway through the project the CPI is .7. To determine the root cause, several stakeholders audit the project and discover tasks were estimated analogously. Although the task estimates add up to the project estimate, the stakeholders think something was missing in how the estimate was completed. Which of the following BEST describes what was missing?

A. Estimated costs should be used to measure CPI

B. SPI should be used, not CPI

C. Bottom up estimating should have been used

D. Past history was not taken into account

QUALITY QUESTIONS

96. A project manager is using a cause-and-effect diagram with the team to determine how various factors might be linked to potential problems. In what step of the quality management process is the project manager involved?

A. Quality analysis

B. Quality assurance

C. Quality control

D. Quality planning

97. **A project manager and team from a firm that designs railroad equipment are tasked to design a machine to load stone onto railroad cars. The design allows for 2% spillage, amounting to over two tons of spilled rock per day. In which of the following does the project manager document quality control, quality assurance, and quality improvements for this project?**

A. Quality management plan

B. Quality policy

C. Control charts

D. Project plan

98. The project team has created a plan describing how they will implement the quality policy. It addresses the organizational structure, responsibilities, procedures, and other information about plans for quality. If this changes during the project, WHICH of the following plans will also change?

A. Quality assurance

B. Quality management

C. Project

D. Quality control

99. You are a project manager for a major information systems project when someone from the quality department comes to see you about beginning a quality audit of your project. The team, already under pressure to complete the project as soon as possible, objects to the audit. You should explain to the team that the purpose of a quality audit is:

A. part of an ISO 9000 investigation.

B. to check if customer is following its quality process.

C. to identify lessons learned that can improve performance on project.

D. to check accuracy of costs submitted by the team.

100. You are in the middle of a major new facility construction project. The structural steel is in place, and the heating conduits are going into place when the project sponsor informs you that he is worried the project will not meet the quality standards. What should you do in this situation?

A. Assure the sponsor that during planning it was determined the project would meet the quality standards

B. Inspect the results so far and use them to determine future results

C. Perform a quality audit

D. Check the results from the last quality management plan

101. You are asked to select tools and techniques to implement a quality assurance program to supplement existing quality control activities. Which of the following would you choose?

A. Quality audits

B. Statistical sampling

C. Pareto diagrams

D. Trend analysis

102. **The new software installation project is in progress. The project manager is working with the quality assurance department to improve everyone's confidence that the project will satisfy the quality standards. Before they can begin this process, which of the following do they need?**

A. Quality problems

B. Quality improvement

C. Quality control measurements

D. Rework

103. **The project you are working on has an increase in cost effectiveness, increased productivity, and increased morale. What might be the reason for these changes?**

A. Project goals are in line with those of the company

B. Increased quality

C. Management's focus on cost containment

D. Rewards presented for individual efforts

104. **A project manager has just taken over the project from another project manager during the execution phase. The previous project manager created a project budget and communication plan and went on to complete other tasks. What should the new project manager do NEXT?**

A. Coordinate performance of work packages

B. Plan for quality

C. Begin risk management

D. Execute the project plan

105. A project is facing a major change to its project deliverables. If the project manager is involved in determining which quality standards are relevant to the change, the project manager must be involved in:

A. quality management.

B. quality assurance.

C. quality planning.

D. quality control.

106. **A project team member comes to the project manager during project execution to tell him that they feel the project cannot meet its quality standards. The project manager calls a meeting of the affected stakeholders to work through the problem. Which step of the quality management process is the project manager in?**

   A. Quality assurance

   B. Quality analysis

   C. Quality control

   D. Quality planning

107. At the end of a project, a project manager determines that the project has added four areas of functionality and three areas of performance. The customer has expressed satisfaction with the project. What does this mean in terms of the success of the project?

A. The project is an unqualified success.

B. The project is unsuccessful because it was gold plated.

C. The project was unsuccessful because the customer being happy means they would have paid more for the work.

D. The project was successful because the team had a chance to learn new areas of functionality and the customer was satisfied.

HUMAN RESOURCE QUESTIONS

108. You have just been assigned as project manager for a large telecommunications project. This one-year project is about halfway done. The project team consists of five sellers and 20 of your company's employees. You want to understand who is responsible for doing what on the project. Where would you find such information?

A. Responsibility matrix

B. Resource histogram

C. Gantt chart

D. Project organization chart

109. During project planning in a matrix organization, the project manager determines that additional human resources are needed. From whom would he request these resources?

A. Project manager

B. Functional manager

C. Team

D. Project sponsor

110. **A project manager must publish a project schedule. Activities, start/end times, and resources are identified. What should the project manager do NEXT?**

A. Distribute the project schedule according to the communications plan

B. Confirm the availability of the resources

C. Refine the project plan to reflect more accurate costing information

D. Publish a Gantt chart illustrating the timeline

111. **During each project team meeting the project manager asks the team member to describe the work he or she is doing, and the project manager assigns new tasks to team members. The length of these meetings has increased because there are many different tasks to assign. This could be happening for all the following reasons EXCEPT?**

A. Lack of a WBS

B. Lack of a responsibility matrix

C. Lack of resource leveling

D. Lack of team involvement in project planning

112. You are a project manager leading a cross-functional project team in a weak matrix environment. None of your project team members report to you functionally and you do not have the ability to directly reward their performance. The project is difficult, involving tight date constraints, and challenging quality standards. Which of the following types of project management power will likely be the MOST effective in this circumstance?

A. Referent

B. Expert

C. Penalty

D. Formal

113. A team member is not performing well on the project because she is inexperienced in system development work. There is no one else available who is better qualified to do the work. What is the BEST solution for the project manager?

A. Consult with the functional manager to determine project completion incentives for the team member

B. Obtain a new resource more skilled in development work

C. Arrange for the team member to get the training

D. Allocate some of the project schedule reserve

114. **A project manager has just found out that a major subcontractor for her project is consistently late delivering work. The project team member responsible for this part of the project does not get along with the subcontractor. To resolve the problem the project manager says, "You both will have to give up something to solve this problem." What conflict resolution mode is she using?**

A. Confrontation

B. Compromise

C. Smoothing

D. Communicating

115. **A project has several teams. Team C has repeatedly missed deadlines in the past. This has caused Team D to have to crash the critical path several times. As the project leader for Team D, you should meet with the:**

A. manager over Team D.

B. project manager alone.

C. project manager and management.

D. project manager and the Team C leader.

116. **On his first project assignment as the project manager, the project manager encounters disagreements among highly technical team members. How would the project manager BEST deal with the conflict?**

A. He should listen to the differences of opinions, determine what is the best choice, and implement that choice.

B. He should postpone further discussions, meet with each individual, and determine the best approach.

C. He should listen to the differences of opinions, encourage logical discussions, and facilitate an agreement.

D. He should help the team focus on agreeable aspects of their opinions and build unity by using relaxation techniques and common focus team building.

117. A project manager has just been hired and is trying to gain the cooperation of others. What is the BEST form of power for gaining cooperation under these circumstances?

A. Formal

B. Referent

C. Penalty

D. Expert

118. A project manager is trying to settle a dispute between two team members. One says the systems should be integrated before testing, and the other maintains each system should be tested before integration. The project involves over 30 people, and 12 systems need to be integrated. The sponsor is demanding that integration happen on time. What is the BEST statement the project manager can make to resolve the conflict?

A. Do it my way.

B. Let's calm down and get the job done.

C. Let's deal with this again next week after we all calm down.

D. Let's test one system after integration and one before integration and see if there are any differences.

119. **You provide a project cost estimate for the project to the project sponsor. He is unhappy with the estimate, because he thinks the price should be lower. He asks you to cut 15% off the project estimate. What should you do?**

   A. Start the project and constantly look for cost savings

   B. Tell all the team members to cut 15% from their estimate

   C. Inform the sponsor of the tasks to be cut

   D. Look for resources with low hourly rates

120. Project information has been distributed according to the communications plan. Some project deliverables have been changed. Those changes were made according to the change control plan. One stakeholder expressed surprise to the project manager upon being informed of a previously published change to a project deliverable. All stakeholders received the communication containing notification of the change. What should the project manager do?

A. Determine why the stakeholder did not receive the information and let him know when it was published

B. Review the communications plan to determine why the stakeholder did not understand his responsibility

C. Review the communications plan and make revisions, if necessary

D. Address the situation in the next steering committee meeting so others do not miss published changes

121. A project team has members in five different locations with varying information systems. The project manager works with the project team to determine how project information will be distributed. These methods are detailed in which document?

A. Overall project plan

B. Scope statement

C. Communication management plan

D. Staffing management plan

122. A large, one-year telecommunications project is about halfway done when you take the place of the previous project manager. The project involves three different sellers and a project team of 30 people. You would like to see the project's communications requirements and what technology is being used to aid in project communications. Where will you find this information?

A. Project plan

B. Information distribution plan

C. Gantt chart

D. Communications management plan

123. **As the project manager, you are preparing your methods for quality management. In your project management system, you are looking for a method that can demonstrate the relationship between events and their resulting effects. You want to use the method to depict the events that cause a negative effect on quality. Which of the following is the BEST choice for accomplishing your objective?**

A. Histogram

B. Pareto chart

C. Ishikawa diagram

D. Control chart

124. **A project manager had a complex problem to solve and made a decision about what needed to be done. A few months later, the problem resurfaced. Most likely what did the project manager not do?**

A. Proper risk analysis

B. Confirm that the decision solved the problem

C. Have the project sponsor validate the decision

D. Use an Ishikawa diagram

125. Communication is key to the success of a project. As the project manager, you have four stakeholders you need to communicate with. As such, you have six channels of communication. A new stakeholder has been added that you also need to communicate with. How many communication channels do you have now?

A. 7

B. 10

C. 12

D. 16

126. **Two people are arguing about what needs to be done to complete a task. If the project manager wants to know what is going on, she should pay MOST attention to:**

A. what is said.

B. what is being discussed according to those arguing.

C. physical mannerisms.

D. the pitch and tone of the voices.

127. **A project manager has a project team consisting of people from four countries. The project is very important to the company and the project manager is concerned about its success. The length of the project schedule is acceptable. What type of communication methods should he/she use?**

A. Informal verbal

B. Formal written

C. Formal verbal

D. Informal written

128. The project status meeting is not going well. Everyone is talking at the same time, there are people who are not participating, and many topics are being discussed at random. Which of the following rules for effective meetings is NOT being adhered to?

A. Courtesy and consideration of each other

B. Schedule meetings in advance

C. Have a purpose for the meeting

D. Create and publish an agenda

129. You have just been assigned as project manager for a large manufacturing project. This one-year project is about halfway done. It involves five different sellers and 20 members of your company on the project team. You want to quickly review where the project now stands. Which of the following reports would be the MOST helpful in finding such information?

A. Task status

B. Progress

C. Forecast

D. Communication

130. **A project manager has just reached the end of a project. Which of the following documents will the project manager need for closure of the project?**

A. Documents that describe the project status

B. Trend analyses

C. Change requests

D. Documents that describe the product of the project

131. **A project manager has just finished the risk response plan for a US $387,000 engineering project. Which of the following should he do NEXT?**

A. Determine the overall risk rating of the project

B. Begin to analyze the risks that show up in the project drawings

C. Add tasks to the project work breakdown structure

D. Hold a project risk review

132. A project manager has asked various stakeholders to determine the probability and impact of a number of risks. He then tested assumptions and evaluated the precision of the risk data. He is about to move to the next step of risk management. Based on this information, what has the project manager forgotten to do?

A. Evaluate trends in risk analysis

B. Identify triggers

C. Provide a standardized risk rating matrix

D. Create a fallback plan

133. **A project manager has assembled the project team, identified 56 risks on the project, determined what would trigger the risks, ranked them on a risk rating matrix, tested their assumptions, and measured the precision of the data used. The team is continuing to move through the risk management process. What has the project manager forgotten?**

A. Simulation

B. Risk mitigation

C. Overall risk ranking for the project

D. Involvement of other stakeholders

134. You are a project manager for a major new manufacturing plant that has never been done before. The project cost is estimated at US $30,000,000 and will make use of three sellers. Once begun, the project cannot be canceled, as there will be a large expenditure on plant and equipment. As the project manager, it would be MOST important to carefully:

A. review all cost proposals from the sellers.

B. examine the budget reserves.

C. complete the project charter.

D. perform an identification of risks.

135. During risk planning, your team cannot come up with an effective way to mitigate or insure against a risk. It is not a task that could be outsourced, nor could it be deleted. What would be the BEST solution?

A. Accept the risk

B. Continue to investigate ways to mitigate the risk

C. Look for ways to avoid the risk

D. Look for ways to transfer the risk

136. **A project manager is quantifying risk for her project. Several of her experts are off-site, but wish to be included in the risk assessment portion of the project. How can this be done?**

A. Use Monte Carlo simulation using the Internet as a tool

B. Apply the critical path method

C. Use informal surveys with known experts

D. Apply the Delphi technique

137. **An experienced project manager has just begun working for a large information technology integrator when the project manager wants to begin to identify all of the project risks. Which of the following would BEST help in this effort?**

A. Her WBS from the project planning phase

B. Her scope statement from project planning phase

C. Her resource plan from project planning phase

D. A conversation with a team member from a similar project that failed in the past

138. You have been appointed as the manager of a new large and complex project. Because this project is business-critical and very visible, the project's executive sponsor has told you to analyze the project's risks and prepare mitigation strategies for them as soon as possible. The organization has risk management procedures that are seldom used or followed, and has had a history of handling risks badly. The project's first milestone is in two weeks. In preparing the plan to manage risks, input from which of the following is generally LEAST important?

A. Project team members

B. Executive sponsor

C. Individuals responsible for risk management policies and templates

D. Key stakeholders

139. You were in the middle of deploying new technology to field offices across the country. A hurricane caused power outages just when the upgrade was near completion. When the power was restored, all of the information was lost, with no way of retrieving it. What should have been done to prevent this?

A. Purchase insurance

B. Plan for a reserve fund

C. Monitor the weather and have a system back-up

D. Schedule the installation outside of the hurricane season

140. A system development project is nearing closure when an unplanned risk is identified. This could potentially affect the project's overall ability to deliver. What should be done NEXT?

    A. Alert the project sponsor of potential impacts to cost, scope, or schedule

    B. Qualify the risk

    C. Mitigate this risk by developing a risk response plan

    D. Develop a workaround

141. The CPI of a project is .6 and the SPI is .71. The project has 625 tasks and is being completed over a four year period. The team members are very inexperienced and the project received little support for proper planning. Which of the following is the BEST thing to do?

A. Update the risk identification and analysis

B. Spend more time improving the cost estimates

C. Remove as many tasks as possible

D. Reorganize the responsibility matrix

PROCUREMENT QUESTIONS

142. **Your program manager has come to you, the project manager, for help with a bid for her newest project. You want to protect your company from financial risk. You have limited scope definition. What type of contract would you choose?**

A. Fixed price contract

B. Cost plus percent of cost contract

C. Time and materials contract

D. Cost-plus fixed fee contract

143. Negotiations between two parties are becoming complex, so party A makes some notes that both parties sign. However, when the work is being done, party B claims that they are not required to provide an item they both agreed to during negotiations, because it was not included in the subsequent contract. In this case, party B is:

A. incorrect because both parties must comply with what they agreed upon.

B. correct because both parties must comply with what they agreed to in the signed contract.

C. generally correct because both parties are only required to perform what is in the contract.

D. generally incorrect because all agreements must be upheld.

144. **Your project has just been fast tracked and you are looking to bring in a subcontractor quickly. There is no time to issue an RFP, so you choose to use a company you have used many times before. A primary concern in this situation is:**

A. collusion between subcontractors.

B. the subcontractor's qualifications.

C. the subcontractor's evaluation criteria.

D. holding a bidders conference.

145. The project manager and project sponsor are discussing the project costs and whether it is better to have their own company do part of the project or hire another company to do the work. If they asked for your opinion, you might say it would be better to do the work yourself if:

A. there is a lot of proprietary data.

B. you had the expertise, but you do not.

C. you felt you needed control over the work.

D. you knew you had the resources to complete your part of the project.

146. A project manager is attending his first bidder's conference and has asked you for advice on what to do during the session. Which of the following is the BEST advice you can give him?

A. You do not need to attend this session; the contract manager will hold it.

B. Watch for sellers who ask too many questions in an attempt to block out the other sellers.

C. Make sure you give all the sellers enough time to ask questions. They may not want to ask questions while their competitors are in the room.

D. Let the project sponsor handle the meeting so you can be the good guy in the negotiation session.

147. **A seller is awarded a contract to build a pipeline. The contract terms and conditions require a work plan be issued for the buyer's approval prior to commencing work but the seller fails to provide one. WHICH of the following should the buyer's project manager do?**

A. File a letter of intent

B. Develop the work plan and issue it to the seller to move things along

C. Issue a default letter

D. Issue a stop work order to the seller until a work plan is prepared

148. **A seller has withdrawn from your project. A new seller has been selected and his/her labor forces are arriving at the job site tomorrow. What is the FIRST thing you should do?**

A. Establish yourself as the authority in charge

B. Bring your team in for introductions and establish a communications exchange

C. Take the new team on a tour of the site and show them where they will be working

D. Bring out the project plan

149. You have just started administrating a contract when management decides to terminate the contract. What should you do FIRST?

A. Go back to solicitation

B. Go back to solicitation planning

C. Finish contract administration

D. Go to contract closure

150. The project team is arguing about the prospective sellers who have submitted proposals. One team member argues for a certain seller while another team member wants the project to be awarded to a different seller. The project manager should remind the team to focus on what item in order to make a selection?

A. Procurement documents

B. Procurement audits

C. Evaluation criteria

D. Procurement management plan

SITUATIONAL AND PROFESSIONAL RESPONSIBILITY

ANSWERS

1. Answer: C

Explanation: Stakeholder management is an ongoing activity that begins in project definition.

Source: PMBOK®, 15

2. Answer: C

Explanation: This type of issue must be settled early in the project because the content and extent of the entire project plan depends on the deliverables and objectives. The best way to resolve the issue is choice C, which is a problem solving method. The other choices are really smoothing or forcing.

Source: PMP® Exam Prep, 23, 141

3. Answer: C

Explanation: "Project management is the application of knowledge, skills, tools, and techniques to project activities to meet project requirements. Project management is accomplished through the use of processes such as: initiating, planning, executing, controlling, and closing." This situation is a recurring process, not a unique project.

Source: PMBOK®, 4-6

4. Answer: C

Explanation: A project coordinator has some authority but management handles important decisions. This is an example of a project coordinator.

Source: PMP® Exam Prep, 44

5. Answer: B

Explanation: The lessons learned are deliverables of the project. The full and satisfactory delivery of project deliverables marks the end of the project.

Source: PMBOK®, 126

6. Answer: C

Explanation: In a publicly traded company, all transactions must be authorized and reported to stockholders using proper accounting standards.

Source: Doing Business Internationally, 210

7. Answer: A

Explanation: Project managers may address unknown risks by applying a general contingency based on past experience.

Source: PMBOK®, 12

8. Answer: C

Explanation: Work out the issue first with the stakeholders. If that fails, then go to the sponsor. Do not add the work without sponsor approval.

Source: PMP® Exam Prep, 26-29

9. Answer: C

Explanation: The direct approach is best.

Source: PMP® Exam Prep, 26

10. Answer: B

Explanation: The only data that definitely tells something is SPI. Less than one is bad, so the project is currently predicted to be behind schedule.

Source: PMP® Exam Prep, 103

11. Answer: A

Explanation: You want to allow everyone to save face and to allow your employee to fix the problem.

Source: PMP® Exam Prep, 26-29

12. Answer: D

Explanation: Choice A will not decrease project costs, just costs over the life of the project. Choice A will not solve the problem. Choice B will almost always lead to higher costs, and choice C could affect costs later.

Source: PMP® Exam Prep, 26

13. Answer: A

Explanation: You need to provide the work as approved by the sponsors. Your input was considered during project initiation.

Source: PMP® Exam Prep, 26-29

14. Answer: C

Explanation: This type of effort is considered routine government action and is therefore not a bribe.

Source: Doing Business Internationally, 210

15. Answer: D

Explanation: Choice D is more ethical and demonstrates good faith.

Source: Doing Business Internationally, 210

16. Answer: B

Explanation: It is your responsibility to keep upper management accurately informed of possible schedule and budget overruns.

Source: PMBOK®, 122

17. Answer: B

Explanation: Because the schedule and scope are already approved, all changes must go through the change control process that was defined during the project planning process.

Source: PMP® Exam Prep, 53

18. Answer: C

Explanation: The request from the customer is a change and should be handled as a change. Choice A and B border on unethical.

Source: PMP® Exam Prep, 51, 208

19. Answer: D

Explanation: Professional responsibility dictates that you should confront the situation first with the other project manager.

Source: PMP® Exam Prep, 26-29

20. Answer: C

Explanation: If your estimates are accurate, management's only options are to reduce scope or quality. Reducing good estimates only gives a false sense of security; as you execute the plan, you will overrun your cost estimates.

Source: PMP® Exam Prep, 98

21. Answer: D

Explanation: Both A and D could have prevented the outcome, but D is the only one that would ensure you were not sitting in a meeting with a document that had not been reviewed.

Source: PMP® Exam Prep, 26-29

22. Answer: B

Explanation: There is no indication that the labor dispute has caused any problems, so there is no need to cease doing business with the company or to pull them off the project. The best choice would be to inform others in your company.

Source: PMP® Exam Prep, 26-29

23. Answer: B

Explanation: You are not empowered to determine the legality of company procedures.

Source: PMP® Exam Prep, 26-29

24. Answer: C

Explanation: Confidential information should be respected (not be disclosed to third parties) without the express approval of the client. See, not all professional responsibility questions are tough!

Source: PMP® Exam Prep, 26-29

25. Answer: B

Explanation: The problem is being resolved because both parties are giving up something. This is a compromise.

Source: PMP® Exam Prep, 143

26. Answer: B

Explanation: The ethical solution is to talk with the customer. You might still be able to win the incentive fee and find a mutually agreeable solution. Think of the good will that will come from telling the customer.

Source: PMP® Exam Prep, 26

27. Answer: A

Explanation: Choices B, C, and D do not solve the problem, they merely postpone it.

Source: PMP® Exam Prep, 26

28. Answer: D

Explanation: Choice C simply withdraws from the problem and is therefore not the best solution. Can you explain why A and B are unethical? The only possible choice is D. That choice would involve quality and other experts to find a resolution.

Source: PMP® Exam Prep, 26

29. Answer: C

Explanation: You should have noticed that only choices A and C involve more people than just the project manager. Since this is an issue involving everyone, everyone should be involved. Choice A may be a good idea in all cases, however, it does not specifically address cultural issues. Therefore, the answer must be C.

Source: PMP® Exam Prep, 26, 61, 152, 154

30. Answer: A

Explanation: There is always a way to decrease costs in the project. How about offering to feature the seller in your next television ad?

Source: PMP® Exam Prep, 202

31. Answer: D

Explanation: You should look for a choice that solves the problem. Choice A is not assertive enough for a project manager. Choice B might be nice but does not address the customer's concerns with the project. Changing the baseline (choice C) is not ethical under these circumstances. You need more information before talking to your manager. Problem solving begins with

defining the causes of the problem.
Therefore, D is the only answer.

Source: PMP® Exam Prep, 156

32. Answer: C

Explanation: Although the deliverable meets
the contractual requirements, it is best to
bring the problem to the customer's
attention so an option that does no harm can
be found.

Source: PMP® Exam Prep, 26, 156

33. Answer: A

Explanation: This is a new project and even
though assessing the range of possible
outcomes is done in a later step, risk
identification should be done first.

Source: PMP® Exam Prep, 176

34. Answer: A

Explanation: This is a non-competitive
procurement. Under these circumstances,
the biggest concern is choice A.

Source: PMP® Exam Prep, 199

35. Answer: B

Explanation: Choice B really means "provide the customer with whatever value you can for the money already spent and stop work." It is ethical to try to provide value or deliverables and not just stop work.

Source: PMP® Exam Prep, 51

36. Answer: A

Explanation: It is the role of the change control board to review and approve changes. That board may include people representative of all of the other choices.

Source: PMP® Exam Prep, 50

37. Answer: A

Explanation: Because an unidentified problem or risk occurred, it is important to perform choices B and C. However, they are not your first choices. You might need to inform management, but this is reactive, not proactive, and not the first thing you should do.

Source: PMP® Exam Prep, 177

38. Answer: A

Explanation: In a way, this is a tough question as there are several viable choices here. However, the project cannot begin without a complete scope of work, so the best answer is A.

Source: PMP® Exam Prep, 194

39. Answer: C

Explanation: Did this one catch you? All deliverables must be quantifiable. The sponsor's deliverable cannot be measured and therefore, needs more work. That means choice A is not correct. All parties rarely agree on all objectives. All the objectives should be met but they must be quantifiable, so choice D is not correct. You need to have more discussions with the sponsor so you can make the objective quantifiable.

Source: PMBOK®, 56

40. Answer: A

Explanation: Choice D will help, but not help both control and deliverables for each phase. Choice C would help control each phase but would not control the integration of the phases into a cohesive whole. Choice B would help improve subsequent phases but would do nothing for control and deliverables. Effective project management requires a life-cycle approach to running the project. Choice A is the only answer that covers both control and deliverables.

Source: PMBOK®, 11

41. Answer: B

Explanation: This situation implies that there are six areas concerned with this project. In addition to added communication requirements, you should be concerned with competing needs and requirements impacting your efforts on configuration management.

Source: PMP® Exam Prep, 24

42. Answer: A

Explanation: Scope definition consists of subdividing major project deliverables (scope) into smaller, more manageable activities. Activity definition defines the activities that must take place to produce those deliverables.

Source: PMBOK®, 57, 67

43. Answer: C

Explanation: Because you have no experience, you will have to look at the experience of others. This information is captured in the historical records of previous projects.

Source: PMP® Exam Prep, 48

44. Answer: D

Explanation: A project manager must manage a project. If all tasks are delegated, chaos ensues and team members will spend more time jockeying for position than completing tasks.

Source: PMBOK® 16

45. Answer: C

Explanation: The steps you should follow are: 1) analyze the situation and impact; 2) develop alternatives with the team; 3) go to management. In this example you need to go through this process before you can explain what will happen to your project.

Source: PMP® Exam Prep, 53

46. Answer: A

Explanation: A single high-level executive can end an entire project if he or she is not satisfied with the results even if that person has, by choice, been only tangentially involved in the project. It is critical to ensure that all of the final decision makers have been identified early in a project in order to ensure that their concerns are addressed.

Source: PMBOK®, 16

47. Answer: D

Explanation: The other impacts to the project should be evaluated first. Such impacts include time, cost, quality, scope of work, and customer satisfaction. Once these are evaluated, the change control board, if one exists, can approve or deny the change.

Source: PMP® Exam Prep, 25

48. Answer: D

Explanation: As you work on a project you need to constantly re-evaluate the project goals and how the project relates to other concurrent projects. Taking into account corporate goals, is your project still in-line with them? If the other project will impact yours, you need to be proactive and work on options now.

Source: PMP® Exam Prep, 67

49. Answer: C

Explanation: Before you can do anything else, you have to know what YOU are going to do. Developing the management strategy will provide the framework for all the rest of these tasks.

Source: PMP® Exam Prep, 23

50. Answer: D

Explanation: First you need to find out why the customer is not happy. Then you meet with the team and determine options.

Source: PMP® Exam Prep, 53

51. Answer: C

Explanation: Document so it becomes part of the historical database.

Source: PMBOK®, 49

52. Answer: D

Explanation: Evaluate the impact to the project, look at options, and then discuss the impact and options with the stakeholders. D is the most correct answer.

Source: PMP® Exam Prep, 53

53. Answer: B

Explanation: You should already have the process for making changes defined before execution of the project. Therefore, if the project manager needs to plan how to make the change, there is no change control system in place.

Source: PMP® Exam Prep, 53

54. Answer: D

Explanation: The team members do not have the same view of the project that you as the project manager have. You see the entire project and can better evaluate with their help the impact of changes to the project.

Source: PMP® Exam Prep, 53

55. Answer: C

Explanation: First you need to understand what change has taken place and then determine the impact and options.

Source: PMP® Exam Prep, 53

56. Answer: D

Explanation: In a decentralized contracting situation there is less focus on maintaining the skill or expertise of the contracting environment.

Source: PMP® Exam Prep, 184

57. Answer: A

Explanation: This is a question that combined the accounting terms in the book PMP® Exam Prep. In order to interpret the information, you need to know what each item is. Based on the information provided, there is no reason to recommend or not recommend project D or C. The BCR for project B is unfavorable. This leaves only project A as providing a clear benefit.

Source: PMP® Exam Prep, 110, 111

58. Answer: B

Explanation: The scope is the basis for making future project decisions and to confirm understanding of the scope among the stakeholders. Since the scope is so important, the project manager must make sure that the needs of all stakeholders are included before continuing the project management process. In order the answer would be choice B, C, A, D.

Source: PMBOK®, 56

59. Answer: B

Explanation: You cannot commit resources without the charter.

Source: PMBOK®, 54

60. Answer: C

Explanation: The charter gives the project manager the authority required to lead the project. It does not describe details of what needs to be done (choice A) or the list of all team members (choice B). These would be in the Project Plan. The project history (choice D) would be in performance reports.

Source: PMP® Exam Prep, 59

61. Answer: D

Explanation: Sometimes the scope of work on a project can be described in great detail. However, sometimes the seller has the expertise and the buyer does little. The scope of work would therefore describe performance or function rather than a complete list of work.

Source: PMP® Exam Prep, 194

62. Answer: A

Explanation: Scope verification must be done at the end of each phase to verify that the work done satisfies the scope of the project.

Source: PMBOK®, 61

63. Answer: A

Explanation: You must meet the needs of your customer. The only issue is that you need to verify that the work you are doing is what the customer wants. Therefore you must still do scope verification at the end of each phase of the project.

Source: PMP® Exam Prep, 66

64. Answer: C

Explanation: In this case you need to bring in the bigger guns. Without scope verification at the end of the project phase, you may well be creating the "wrong thing." This is where management can protect the project.

Source: PMP® Exam Prep, 66

65. Answer: D

Explanation: Ideally there is a change control system in place that should be followed to make changes in the project.

Source: PMP® Exam Prep, 53

66. Answer: C

Explanation: The project deliverables are defined in scope planning.

Source: PMBOK®, 52

67. Answer: D

Explanation: This is a clarification of the project charter and therefore must be addressed to the sponsor who approved the charter.

Source: PMP® Exam Prep, 53

68. Answer: A

Explanation: The question implies finish-to-finish relationships between tasks. Arrow diagramming method does not support these types of relationships.

Source: PMBOK®, 69

69. Answer: B

Explanation: The sequence is neither mandatory nor driven by an external source.

Source: PMP® Exam Prep, 75

70. Answer: D

Explanation: The two paths you have in this question are 1-2-3 and 1-4. Path 1-2-3 would take 1+4+5 days or 10 days to complete. Path 1-4 would take 1+10 days or 11 days to complete. Carefully draw the network diagram, list all the possible paths, and then determine how much time each path would take.

Source: PMP® Exam Prep, 76

71. Answer: B

Explanation: By the time this activity is taking place, initiation, scope definition, and activity sequencing would be completed.

Source: PMP® Exam Prep, 72

72. Answer: C

Explanation: The critical path is ACEF and 107 long. Path BC was 55 long and with the change is now 67 long. Changing task B will have no effect on the critical path.

Source: PMP® Exam Prep, 76

73. Answer: A

Explanation: All the items, except choice A, are part of schedule control and occur after schedule development.

Source: PMBOK®, 66

74. Answer: D

Explanation: Answer D is the MOST correct answer.

Source: PMP® Exam Prep, 86

75. Answer: B

Explanation: PERT uses a weighted average to compute activity durations.

Source: PMBOK®, 75

76. Answer: C

Explanation: Choice A is the same thing as create a network diagram. Choice B is done during control, not during planning. Since a schedule is an input to risk management, choice D comes after choice C and so it is not the "next thing to do." The only remaining choice is C.

Source: PMP® Exam Prep, 31

77. Answer: D

Explanation: The question is really asking, "What is done after activity duration estimating?" A and B are done before activity duration estimating. Duration compression occurs before finalizing the schedule, and it is, therefore, the best answer.

Source: PMBOK®, 73

78. Answer: D

Explanation: The question is really asking, "What is done after activity duration estimating?" All the activities listed, except choice D are done before activity duration estimating.

Source: PMBOK®, 66

79. Answer: A

Explanation: They are using a mathematical model to predict the duration of the task. In this case the model is as simple as just taking the average of all past tasks. Using models is a characteristic of parametric estimates.

Source: PMP® Exam Prep, 100

80. Answer: D

Explanation: A task is probably not on the critical path if there is slack.

Source: PMP® Exam Prep, 76

81. Answer: B

Explanation: Cutting resources from a task (choice A) will not save time nor would moving resources (choice C). Removing a task from the project is a possibility but since the dependencies are preferential and the risk is low, the best choice would be to make more tasks concurrent.

Source: PMP® Exam Prep, 75, 84

82. Answer: A

Explanation: Schedule management is a responsibility of the project manager.

Source: PMBOK®, 79

83. Answer: D

Explanation: Milestone reports present the right level of detail for upper management. You and your team need to understand and use details.

Source: PMP® Exam Prep, 88

84. Answer: A

Explanation: In using NPV the number of years is not relevant. It is already included in the calculation. You simply pick the project with the highest NPV.

Source: PMP® Exam Prep, 109

85. Answer: C

Explanation: Remember the internal rate of return is like the interest rate you get from the bank. The higher the rate the better the return.

Source: PMP® Exam Prep, 110

86. Answer: B

Explanation: You should pick the higher number.

Source: PMP® Exam Prep, 111

87. Answer: D

Explanation: You consider the project length when computing NPV. You would choose the project that provides the most value, in this case the project with the highest NPV.

Source: PMP® Exam Prep, 109

88. Answer: D

Explanation: Procedures for the rental and purchase of supplies and equipment are found in the organizational policies.

Source: PMBOK®, 75

89. Answer: A

Explanation: Analogous estimating is a form of expert judgment.

Source: PMBOK®, 72

90. Answer: B

Explanation: The project budget is created during the planning phase and is part of the project plan deliverable.

Source: PMBOK®, 89

91. Answer: C

Explanation: Choice A is too general. The estimates are already created in this example, so the answer is not B. The answer is not D, cost control, because the baseline has not been created. The correct answer is C.

Source: PMBOK®, 89

92. Answer: B

Explanation: Choice B (sunk cost) should not be considered when deciding whether to continue with a troubled project.

Source: PMP® Exam Prep, 112

93. Answer: A

Explanation: A project without a charter is a project without support. The information provided for the other projects does not justify selecting them. Even the number of resources is not relevant since the number of resources for the new project is not supplied.

Source: PMP® Exam Prep, 59, 109-112

94. Answer: C

Explanation: To answer this question you need to determine which answer could negatively affect both time and cost. Choice A would most likely affect only cost. Choices B and D would most likely affect only schedule.

Source: PMP® Exam Prep, 103

95. Answer: C

Explanation: Actual costs are used to measure CPI, and there's no reason to use

SPI in this situation, so choices A and B are not correct. Using past history is another way of saying "analogous." The best way to estimate is bottom up. Such estimating would have improved the overall quality of the estimate.

Source: PMP® Exam Prep, 100, 103

96. Answer: D

Explanation: The topic has potential problems. They must, therefore, be in quality planning.

Source: PMBOK®, 98

97. Answer: A

Explanation: B and C are components of a quality management plan. The quality plan is part of the project plan. The best answer is the quality management plan.

Source: PMBOK®, 99

98. Answer: C

Explanation: The plan described is the quality management plan. Changing this plan will also change the project plan as it is included as part of a project plan.

Source: PMBOK®, 99

99. Answer: C

Explanation: PMI®'s definition of an audit is different from what we are used to. An audit is a structured review of quality activities to identify lessons learned. These lessons are used for process improvement.

Source: PMP® Exam Prep, 127

100. Answer: C

Explanation: A quality audit helps to prove that quality standards will be met.

Source: PMP® Exam Prep, 127

101. Answer: A

Explanation: Choice A is a structured review of other quality management activities performed to identify lessons learned that can be applied to this and other projects. The other choices are tools and techniques that apply to quality control rather than quality assurance.

Source: PMBOK®, 101

102. Answer: C

Explanation: There's only one choice that makes sense, and that's an official input to quality assurance, C.

Source: PMBOK® , 96

103. Answer: B

Explanation: As you increase quality there
will be associated benefits for the project.
Some of these benefits are increased
productivity, increased cost effectiveness,
decreased cost risk, and improved morale.

Source: PMP® Exam Prep, 126

104. Answer: B

Explanation: Quality planning can occur
during execution of the project. In this
example, the previous project manager did
not complete some of the planning
activities. The new project manager needs
to complete these planning activities.

Source: PMP® Exam Prep, 31

105. Answer: C

Explanation: Although quality planning
usually occurs during planning, it can occur
during execution if there is a change.

Source: PMP® Exam Prep, 127

106. Answer: A

Explanation: Determining if the quality standards are valid is part of the quality assurance process.

Source: PMBOK®, 101

107. Answer: B

Explanation: Gold plating a project wastes time and probably cost. It makes the project unsuccessful.

Source: PMP® Exam Prep, 123

108. Answer: A

Explanation: The responsibility "assignment" matrix maps who will do the work; whereas the resource histogram shows the number of resources used in each time period. In its pure sense, a Gantt chart shows only task and calendar date.

Source: PMP® Exam Prep, 140

109. Answer: B

Explanation: Did you forget that in a matrix organization, the functional manager controls the resources?

Source: PMP® Exam Prep, 39

110. Answer: B

Explanation: The project schedule remains preliminary until resource assignments are confirmed.

Source: PMBOK®, 73

111. Answer: C

Explanation: Resource leveling refers to maintaining the same number of resources on the project for each time period. It has nothing to do with assigning tasks or managing meetings.

Source: PMP® Exam Prep, 140

112. Answer: B

Explanation: Per PMI®, reward and expert are the best sources of power. Here, reward is not an option for you.

Source: PMP® Exam Prep, 141

113. Answer: C

Explanation: The job of the project manager includes providing project specific training. Though the team member's boss might be involved, the project manager should not complain. In many instances team training is a direct cost of the project.

Source: PMBOK®, 116

114. Answer: B

Explanation: The act of both parties giving something defines compromise.

Source: PMP® Exam Prep, 143

115. Answer: D

Explanation: Those having the problem should resolve the problem in PMI®'s view. In this case, the two team leads need to meet, and because it is impacting the project, the project manager needs to participate.

Source: PMP® Exam Prep, 142

116. Answer: C

Explanation: Problem solving and compromising are the two most important conflict resolution techniques. A key general management skill includes conflict management.

Source: PMP® Exam Prep, 143

117. Answer: A

Explanation: Generally the best forms of power are reward or expert. The project manager has not had time to become a recognized expert in the company and reward is not a choice. This leaves formal power as the only logical choice.

Source: PMP® Exam Prep, 141

118. Answer: D

Explanation: Choice D is an example of compromising—one of the best choices for resolving conflict.

Source: PMP® Exam Prep, 143

119. Answer: C

Explanation: This is a major problem in any project when management does not understand project management. Why cut all tasks as in choice B? One should only look at the critical path tasks. Choice A is not correct, because the project manager must deal with the cost problem during planning, not wait until later.

Source: PMP® Exam Prep, 98

120. Answer: C

Explanation: The receiver should make sure communications are received in their entirety and understood.

Source: PMBOK®, 123

121. Answer: C

Explanation: Communication requirements from all locations must be compiled and documented in the communication management plan. This is a part of the overall project plan.

Source: PMBOK®, 120

122. Answer: D

Explanation: Although the information is found as a sub plan to the project plan, the communications management plan is the best answer.

Source: PMP® Exam Prep, 149

123. Answer: C

Explanation: Ishikawa diagrams are also called cause-and-effect diagrams. They illustrate how factors are linked to effects.

Source: PMBOK®, 98

124. Answer: B

Explanation: The steps of problem solving include: implement a decision, review it and confirm that the decision solved the problem.

Source: PMP® Exam Prep, 156

125. Answer: B

Explanation: The formula is (n x (n-1))/2 or (5 x 4)/2 = 10.

Source: PMP® Exam Prep, 156

126. Answer: C

Explanation: Choice C refers to nonverbal communication, which is the most important aspect of a conversation.

Source: PMP® Exam Prep, 152

127. Answer: B

Explanation: Because of the differences in culture and the distance between team members, you need to have formal written communication.

Source: PMP® Exam Prep, 153

128. Answer: D

Explanation: If one has an agenda issued beforehand, people will be following the outline and should not need random decisions.

Source: PMP® Exam Prep, 155

129. Answer: B

Explanation: The key word is quickly. The progress report will summarize project status. The task status is too detailed for a quick look. A forecast report only looks into the future.

Source: PMP® Exam Prep, 156

130. Answer: D

Explanation: Product verification is accomplished in the closure phase. To do the verification, you need the original description to compare to the results.

Source: PMP® Exam Prep, 31, 157

131. Answer: C

Explanation: It is important to note that the risk management process will cause additional tasks to be added to the project. These tasks cost money and time but will reduce the overall cost and time for the project. Choice D occurs during risk monitoring and control, choice A during qualification, and choice B should have already been done.

Source: PMP® Exam Prep, 175

132. Answer: C

Explanation: The activities of qualitative risk analysis are probability and impact definition, assumption testing, data precision ranking, and risk ranking matrix development.

Source: PMP® Exam Prep, 168-9

133. Answer: D

Explanation: The process they have used so far is fine except the input of other stakeholders is needed in order to identify risks.

Source: PMP® Exam Prep, 166

134. Answer: D

Explanation: Though a charter and good cost proposals are important, a risk identification would be the most proactive response and also have the greatest positive impact on the project.

Source: PMP® Exam Prep, 166

135. Answer: A

Explanation: This question relates real world situations to the risk types. Based on the question you cannot delete the task to avoid it, nor can you insure or outsource to transfer the risk. The BEST answer would be to accept the risk.

Source: PMP® Exam Prep, 172

136. Answer: D

Explanation: The Delphi Technique is most commonly used to obtain expert opinions on technical issues, the necessary scope of work, or the risks. This technique ensures anonymity.

Source: PMBOK®, 132

137. Answer: D

Explanation: The best source of knowledge would be reviewing documented impressions with a person on a similar project that failed. This interview would be part of the information gathering to identify risks.

Source: PMBOK®, 132

138. Answer: B

Explanation: The executive sponsor generally is not available for these planning meetings and does not have an intimate knowledge of risk management planning.

Source: PMBOK®, 130

139. Answer: C

Explanation: Avoiding an uncontrollable risk factor by scheduling the installation at a different time could have a large impact on the project schedule. The best choice would be to have a backup.

Source: PMBOK®, 141

140. Answer: B

Explanation: A workaround (choice D) is an unplanned response to risk that is occurring. You could not mitigate the risk (choice C) until you qualified the risk. You would need to analyze the problem before you would talk to the sponsor (choice A).

Source: PMBOK®, 146

141. Answer: A

Explanation: The PMBOK® says, "When the project deviates significantly from the baseline, updated risk identification and analysis should be performed."

Source: PMBOK®, 145

142. Answer: D

Explanation: Of the options given, the only contract that limits fees for large projects with limited scope definition is cost plus fixed fee.

Source: PMBOK®, 151

143. Answer: B

Explanation: You are only required to deliver what is defined in the contract.

Source: PMP® Exam Prep, 184

144. Answer: B

Explanation: Although you have used this contractor before, how can you be sure they are qualified to do the new work unless it is exactly like previous work? This is the risk you are taking.

Source: PMP® Exam Prep, 189

145. Answer: A

Explanation: It is generally better to do the work yourself if using an outside company means you have to turn over highly confidential proprietary data to the other company.

Source: PMP® Exam Prep, 187

146. Answer: C

Explanation: One of the things to watch out for is a seller who does not ask questions. The sponsor does not hold the meeting (choice D), the project manager must be present (choice A), and a seller's evaluation form does not exist.

Source: PMP® Exam Prep, 200

147. Answer: C

Explanation: Any time that a seller does not perform according to the contract, the project manager must take action. The preferred choice might be to contact the seller and ask what is going on, but that choice is not available here. Therefore, the best choice is to let him know he is in default.

Source: PMP® Exam Prep, 197

148. Answer: A

Explanation: The best answer here is to establish roles and responsibilities for the project.

Source: PMP® Exam Prep, 203

149. Answer: D

Explanation: If the contract is terminated, the project needs to enter closure.

Source: PMP® Exam Prep, 210

150. Answer: C

Explanation: The evaluation criteria is the primary tool for evaluating potential sellers and should be used by the entire team in order to make a selection.

Source: PMBOK®, 155

BIBLIOGRAPHY

Rita Mulcahy PMP, *PMP® Exam Prep*;
ISBN 0-9711647-0-3
RMC Publications, 2001

Project Management Institute, *A Guide to
the Project Management Body of
Knowledge PMBOK® Guide 2000 Edition*;
ISBN 1-880410-23-0
Project Management Institute, 2000

Terence Brake, *Doing Business
Internationally, The Guide to Cross-
Cultural Success;*
ISBN 0-7863-0117-1
McGraw Hill, 1995